D1153176

MY CHRISTMAS BOOK
of Stories and Carols

Linda Jennings

illustrated by

Anne Grahame Johnstone

AWARD PUBLICATIONS

ISBN 1-84135-307-8

Copyright © 1990 Award Publications Limited

First published 1990
This edition first published 2004

Published by Award Publications Limited,
27 Longford Street, London NW1 3DZ

Printed in Malaysia

Contents

The Christmas Story	4
The Angel's Visit	4
Christ's Birth	5
The Shepherds on the Hill	6
The Three Wise Men	8
The Flight into Egypt	10
Coventry Carol	10
Barney's Pony	11
The Hurdy Gurdy Man	12
Amos's Lamb	14
Deck the Halls	16
The Holly and the Ivy	16
The Children's Christmas	18
The Twelve Days of Christmas	20
The Robin's Carol	22
Polly's Pets	23
Christmas Decorations	25
A Present from Norway	26
King Wenceslaus	28
Silent Night	29
Tree in the Moonlight	30
The Christmas Crib	32
St Nicholas	34
The Mistletoe Kiss	35
I Saw Three Ships	37
The Christmas Surprise	38
Away in a Manger	40
Lucy's Mistake	41
The Christmas Parcel Disaster	42
Martin Luther and the Candles	44
Once in Royal David's City	45
The Birds' Christmas	46
God Rest Ye Merry, Gentlemen	48
The Magic Toyshop	50
Here We Come A-Wassailing	52
Jack Frost	53
The Young King's Gift	54
In the Bleak Midwinter	56
Acknowledgements	57

The Christmas Story

The Angel's Visit

Long ago in Nazareth there lived a girl called Mary. She was gentle and modest, and was engaged to a carpenter named Joseph. Although Joseph was much older than Mary she was looking forward to her marriage, for Joseph was a kind man and a skilled craftsman. Mary knew he would make a good and considerate husband.

One day, when Mary was walking in the countryside, something very strange happened to her, something that would affect the whole world from that time onwards. Mary was suddenly bathed in a dazzling light, so strong that at first she hid her face from it. When she ventured to look up she found herself gazing at a shining, beautiful figure. She knew she was looking at an angel.

'Do not be afraid, Mary,' said the angel. 'My name is Gabriel and I have been sent from God with a special message for you.'

Mary trembled. What could such a heavenly being have to say to her, Mary, a mere village girl? What had she done to bring such a visitor to earth?

'You will bear a son,' went on the angel. 'Although you will marry Joseph your son will not be his child. Joseph will be his earthly father, but He will be born the Son of God. You will call Him Jesus, for He will be the Saviour of the World.'

Mary could hardly take it in. The coming of God's son had been foretold for generations. How strange and wonderful that *she* was chosen to become the mother of the Son of God!

She bowed her head. 'So be it,' she said. 'It is God's will.'

When she looked up again Gabriel had gone. But within her she felt a great surge of joy, and she ran all the way down the hillside to tell the news to Joseph.

Now Joseph knew Mary to be entirely truthful and not given to fanciful dreams. When he saw her face and the joy that shone from it he knew she was telling the truth.

Together they planned their forthcoming marriage.

Christ's Birth

Every year Joseph had to travel to Bethlehem in Judea to pay his taxes. It was a long journey, and this particular year Joseph was very worried because his wife Mary's baby was nearly due.

'It would be best for you to stay behind, Mary,' he said gently.

But Mary needed Joseph by her side when the baby came, so she insisted on accompanying him. Joseph saddled the donkey and Mary sat on it while he walked by her side. She looked pale and tired, but her face shone with an inner light as the day approached when she would bear God's son.

At last Mary and Joseph reached Bethlehem. It was a cold frosty night and the stars shone brightly. Because they had arrived so late they found that every single inn was fully booked.

Joseph knew that Mary needed shelter and warmth for the birth of her baby.

'We'll try this last inn,' he sighed, but without much hope. Bethlehem was brimming with people like themselves, who had all come to pay their taxes.

The innkeeper shook his head as Joseph asked for a bed. 'The last one was taken an hour ago,' he said, starting to close the door.

'Oh, please,' said Mary. 'Have you nowhere at all? My baby will be born soon, and he must have shelter.'

The innkeeper shone his lantern into the young girl's face. She looked exhausted and now sat uncomfortably on the donkey, her head bowed.

The innkeeper was moved with pity. He rubbed his chin and thought hard.

'There's the stable at the back of the inn,' he said. 'If you don't mind sharing it with the cattle, you are welcome to stay there.'

Joseph thanked him warmly and the little party made their way to the stable, which was really a cave carved into the hillside. They found themselves a corner and lay down on the sweet-smelling hay.

Later that night Mary had her baby. She wrapped him in some warm blankets she had brought with her and, because she had no cradle, she laid him gently in the manger.

The night that Jesus, Son of God, was born the world lay sleeping. All was silent in the stable, save for the lowing of the cattle and the cooing of the doves in the rafters. Mary looked down on her tiny son, wondering what the world would hold for Him.

The Shepherds on the Hill

Outside the town of Bethlehem some shepherds were tending their flocks on the hillside. Sometimes these winter nights seemed very long and cold, for there was little to do but huddle round a fire while one of the shepherds kept watch for wolves and sheep-stealers.

This particular night, though, there seemed to be an air of excitement. Perhaps it was the many people they had seen wending their way to the little town. Perhaps it was the stars in the velvet-black sky which shone and sparkled more brightly than they had ever seen them. Suddenly a light appeared that was stronger than the brightest star. The shepherds were so frightened that they flung themselves to the ground, covering their heads.

'Do not be afraid,' came a voice from above them. 'For it is good news that I bring.'

One shepherd cautiously raised his head. A bright and beautiful angel stood there, and it was he who had spoken.

'Go all of you into Bethlehem, for in a stable tonight the Son of God has been born.'

The shepherds all rose to their feet and saw to their amazement a great throng of angels in the sky, singing and giving praise to God for the miracle of this birth.

When the angels had gone the head shepherd said to the others:

'Come, we must go into the town to find this baby. For if angels have appeared to us to tell us the news, then surely He must be the Son of God.'

The shepherds hurried down the hillside, the youngest shepherd clutching a lamb that had just been born. 'We must take the baby a gift,' he said.

They had no difficulty in finding the stable, for Joseph's lantern shone out into the night, and the shepherds could see the couple, bending over the manger where the child lay.

They gathered round and marvelled at the tiny child, so peacefully sleeping, who was to become the Saviour of them all.

The Three Wise Men

To the east of Bethlehem, in a far-off country, there lived three wise men. They read many learned books, and they studied the stars. When a new star appeared in the sky and when they learned that it shone over Judea they became very excited.

'It has been foretold by the prophets that an important king will be born in Bethlehem in Judea. And now we have the sign!'

The Wise Men hastily packed their belongings and each bought a costly gift for the young king. Then they saddled their camels and set off on the long journey westwards, following the new star to guide them on their way.

First they came to Jerusalem.

Now Herod the King ruled in Jerusalem, and when he heard of the three strangers who were searching for the new king he felt afraid. If there was a new king who had a special star to announce his birth, then he must be very great indeed. What would happen to him, King Herod?

Herod called the Wise Men to his palace and questioned them about the baby.

'He is born in Bethlehem,' said one of the Wise Men. 'For so it has been told by the prophets. This baby will be the greatest king the world has ever known.'

It was as he feared. Herod knew that somehow this baby must be destroyed.

'I, too, will want to visit this new king,' he told the Wise Men. 'When you return to your country, come to Jerusalem first and tell me exactly where he can be found so that I may go there to worship him.'

The Wise Men promised they would, and they left Jerusalem following the star all the way to Bethlehem. There it shone right over the stable, illuminating Mary, Joseph, and the young Jesus who Mary held in her arms.

The Wise Men saw greatness in the tiny child, and they bowed down on their knees to worship him.

Then they presented Him with their gifts, gold, frankincense, and myrrh.

'Now we must go back to tell Herod where the young king may be found,' said one of the Wise Men, but that night they all had a dream. They were warned that if they told Herod where Jesus was, the jealous king would go to Bethlehem and kill him.

So the three Wise Men returned to their country by another route.

The Flight into Egypt

That night Joseph, too, had a dream. An angel appeared to him and told him to take Mary and Jesus all the way to Egypt.

'For Herod the King will come to Bethlehem and he will search for Jesus and kill him.'

Joseph woke Mary and together they gathered together their belongings. Mary looked fondly at her little sleeping son. How could anyone wish to harm such a young and helpless child? But Mary knew even then that Jesus's life would not be easy. There would be too many people in the world who would be jealous of his goodness and his power. She held him tight, wondering what the future would bring.

Meanwhile, in Jerusalem, Herod waited and waited for the return of the Wise Men. When he finally realised that they had no intention of coming back to tell him where the baby was to be found he was very, very angry.

He made a terrible decision. He sent soldiers into Bethlehem who were given orders to kill every male child under two years old. But though there was much weeping and great sorrow in Bethlehem when the soldiers had done their dreadful deeds, Jesus was safe in Egypt with his parents.

A few years later Herod died, and an angel told Joseph it was safe to return home to their own country.

So the little family came back to Nazareth where the young Christ Child grew up, helping Joseph in his carpenter's shop.

Coventry Carol

Lullay, lullay, thou little tiny child,
Bye bye, lully, lullay,
Lully, lullay, thou tiny child,
Bye bye, lully, lullay.

O sisters too, how may we do,
For to preserve this day
This poor youngling for whom we sing
Bye bye, lully, lullay?

Herod the king in his raging,
Chargèd he hath this day
His men of might, in his own sight,
All children young to slay.

Then woe is me, poor child, for thee,
And ever morn and day
For Thy parting nor say nor sing
Bye bye, lully, lullay.

Barney's Pony

Barney had a pony. It was called Muffin, and Barney loved it very much and groomed it every single day.

His brother Stephen was very scornful of Barney's pony. 'It's too small to be of any use,' he scoffed. 'It can't jump fences, and it's too fat to win any races.'

Barney didn't care. His pony could trot steadily along the lanes and he was great company. Who wanted to win races?

But Stephen's teasing didn't stop. Even Mama and Papa laughed at Muffin sometimes.

'He should be called Barrel,' said Papa.

That Christmas it snowed and snowed. Papa kept looking out of the window as the snow grew deeper and deeper.

'If it doesn't stop,' he said, 'I won't be able to drive the carriage to Grandmama's with the presents.'

Every Christmas Eve Barney's parents would take presents over to Grandmama. She liked to open them on Christmas Eve, because that's what they used to do, long ago, when she was a little girl in Germany. Then on Christmas Day she would come over to Barney's house to lunch.

But this Christmas it looked as if Grandmama would go without her presents and her lunch.

'She'll be so disappointed,' said Mama.

Barney suddenly had an idea. 'We could use Muffin,' he said.

Stephen burst out laughing. 'Ho, ho! That Christmas pudding on legs. What can he do?'

'I'll take the presents over on Christmas Eve,' said Barney. 'Muffin doesn't mind the snow. Then Papa can walk with Muffin to Grandmama's the next day and bring her back to lunch on Muffin's back.'

Stephen stopped laughing and Mama and Papa thought hard.

'So long as you get back before dark,' said Mama.

'And keep to the path,' said Papa. 'You can still see the track.'

So Barney set out to Grandmama's cottage, riding Muffin, and laden with presents.

And on Christmas morning Grandmama hitched up her best dress and sat astride Muffin as Papa led them back home for Christmas lunch!

The Hurdy Gurdy Man

'It's not much like Christmas when there's no snow,' complained Edmund. He looked gloomily out of the window on to the London street.

Mary came to the window and looked out. Edmund was right. It didn't look Christmassy at all, and there were even a few brown leaves clinging to the trees.

'Listen,' cried Edmund suddenly. 'Can you hear it?'

Mary opened the window and leaned out. It didn't even feel cold. But down the street she could see a familiar sight.

'The hurdy-gurdy man!' she cried.

'And he's playing Christmas carols,' exclaimed Edmund excitedly. 'Let's go out to meet him.'

Both children raced down the long staircase without even putting on their coats. When they reached the street they found other children already there, to greet the hurdy-gurdy man and his little monkey.

And they all danced round the barrel-organ to the sound of 'The Holly and the Ivy.'

'*Now* it feels like Christmas!' said Mary.

Amos's Lamb

More than anything in the world Amos loved his little white and black lamb, Jacob. One night, earlier that winter, Father had saved the lamb from a wolf. He had brought it back home, injured, and Amos had nursed it until it was completely well again. Now the lamb followed Amos everywhere. Amos just couldn't imagine life without his lamb.

At the end of the year, in the very coldest part of the winter, something very special happened. Amos's father was out with the other shepherds, guarding his sheep from wolves and robbers, while Amos, who was still too young to go with his father, was sleeping peacefully at home. Suddenly the little boy was woken by a bright light which shone through the doorway of the hut. Amos reached out to touch the warm woolly fur of his lamb which lay sleeping beside him. He was very frightened.

Suddenly his father burst into the room, his eyes shining with excitement. 'Get up, Amos,' he ordered. 'Something wonderful has happened!'

Amos rubbed the sleep from his eyes. 'What, Father?'

'We have been visited by angels,' he said. 'They tell us that the great king, promised by the prophets, has been born here, in Bethlehem.'

A king? Angels? Here in Bethlehem? Amos's mouth dropped open in surprise.

'Come along now,' said his father, pulling Amos to his feet. 'Think, Amos, we will be the first people on this earth to pay homage to the King of Israel!'

'Can Jacob come too?' asked Amos. To go to see such a wonderful thing without his lamb would be unthinkable.

Father smiled. 'Yes, he can come too.'

As they hurried along to the stable where the baby Jesus was lying, Amos suddenly felt small and poor. 'I should give the baby a present, Father,' he said. 'But I haven't anything to give.'

Father looked at him. 'Yes, you have, Amos,' he said.

Amos gave a little cry. 'Oh no, Father, not Jacob! Not my little lamb! I'll never part with Jacob!' But when Amos approached the stable and saw the manger with the Christ Child lying in it, he felt ashamed.

He has nothing at all, he thought. He's even poorer than I am. He'd love Jacob, I know he would. He stood for a moment, fighting back the tears. Then the little shepherd boy led his lamb to the manger and smiled up at Mary.

'I've brought Him a lamb,' he said.

Mary looked into Amos's eyes and saw the pain in them as he parted with the creature he loved the most in the whole world.

'Little shepherd,' she said gently. 'You need your lamb. My Son would not wish you to grieve, I know that.'

The tiny child reached out and grasped Jacob's woolly nose.

'Your love is all my Son needs,' she went on. 'You have given Him that by offering Him your lamb. Go home, little boy, and take your precious lamb with you.'

Later, as Amos walked back up the hillside with his lamb, he noticed something. Where the Babe had clutched at Jacob's nose there now grew a patch of pure white wool, shaped like a tiny star.

Deck the Halls

Deck the halls with boughs of holly,
Fa la la la la, fa la la la.
'Tis the season to be jolly,
Fa la la la la, fa la la la.
Don we now our gay apparel,
Fa la la, fa la la, la la la.
Troll the ancient Yuletide carol,
Fa la la la la, fa la la la.

See the blazing Yule before us,
Strike the harp and join the chorus,
Follow me in merry measure,
While I tell of Yuletide treasure.

Fast away the old year passes,
Hail the new, ye lads and lasses,
Sing we joyous all together,
Heedless of the wind and weather.

The Holly and the Ivy

The holly and the ivy,
When they are both full grown,
Of all the trees that are in the wood,
The holly bears the crown:

*Oh, the rising of the sun
And the running of the deer,
The playing of the merry organ,
Sweet singing in the choir.*

The holly bears a blossom,
As white as the lily flower,
And Mary bore sweet Jesus Christ
To be our sweet Saviour:

The holly bears a berry
As red as any blood,
And Mary bore sweet Jesus Christ
To do us sinners good:

The holly bears a prickle,
As sharp as any thorn,
And Mary bore sweet Jesus Christ,
On Christmas Day in the morn:

The holly bears a bark,
As bitter as any gall,
And Mary bore sweet Jesus Christ
For to redeem us all:

The holly and the ivy,
When they are both full grown,
Of all the trees that are in the wood,
The holly bears the crown:

The Children's Christmas

It was to have been the best Christmas ever, but it nearly turned out to be the worst.

Uncle Ken and Aunt Amy were coming for Christmas lunch, and the children were looking forward to it. They all loved Aunt Amy, with her infectious laugh and funny jokes, and Uncle Ken, who always had a treat or two tucked away in his pocket.

Then, on Christmas morning, disaster struck. Father, who was a doctor, was suddenly called out to a patient.

Mother was just putting the turkey in the oven when she put her hand to her head and said to the children:

'Oh dear, I don't really feel very well. I think it may be the flu.'

'You should go to bed,' said Rebecca, who was the eldest. 'I'll get you a hot-water bottle.'

'I can't go to bed,' wailed Mother. 'Who on earth would cook and serve the lunch?'

'*We* can,' said Sophie firmly, though William looked very doubtful.

'But there's the turkey and the vegetables and the Christmas pudding and the jellies. How on earth can you do all that? You'll never manage…'

'Of *course* we'll manage,' said Rebecca. 'Sophie can make lovely jellies, and I'll light the Christmas pudding. As for the turkey – why, it's nearly cooked, so there's little to do there. Uncle Ken can carve it for us.'

'What about me,' wailed little Mattie. 'I want to help too.'

'Oh, you can arrange all the sweets and nuts and things on little dishes,' said Rebecca. She went to the stove to boil up a kettle for her mother's hot-water bottle.

'Now, off you go to bed,' she ordered. 'Don't worry, Mother, we'll manage all right!'

And manage they did. When Uncle Ken and Aunt Amy arrived all four children were washed, dressed and ready with the Christmas lunch! Sophie had even made Mother some soup which she put in a bowl on a tray, with a sprig of holly in a vase.

Father arrived home just as the procession of children was making its way to the table with the Christmas pudding and other goodies.

'Don't worry, Father,' said William gaily. 'Your turkey's in the oven piping hot – with all the trimmings, too!'

'Everything all right?' asked Mother, who was sitting up in bed looking a little better. 'Oh, Sophie, one of your special jellies – I think I may be able to manage a little of that!'

Later Mother heard the sound of carols drifting up from the sitting-room. She lay back on the pillows and smiled. 'Not *quite* the best Christmas ever, but very nearly so!' she said to herself.

The Twelve Days of Christmas

On the first day of Christmas my true love sent to me
A partridge in a pear tree.

On the second day of Christmas my true love sent to me
Two turtle doves and a partridge in a pear tree.

On the third day of Christmas my true love sent to me
Three French hens, two turtle doves, and a partridge
in a pear tree.

On the fourth day of Christmas my true love sent to me
Four calling birds, three French hens, two turtle doves,
and a partridge in a pear tree.

On the fifth day of Christmas my true love sent to me
Five gold rings, four calling birds, three French hens,
two turtle doves and a partridge in a pear tree.

On the sixth day of Christmas my true love sent to me
Six geese a-laying, five gold rings, four calling birds,
three French hens, two turtle doves, and a partridge
in a pear tree.

On the seventh day of Christmas my true love sent to me
Seven swans a-swimming, six geese a-laying, five gold rings,
four calling birds, three French hens, two turtle doves,
and a partridge in a pear tree.

On the eighth day of Christmas my true love sent to me
Eight maids a-milking, seven swans a-swimming, six geese
a-laying, five gold rings, four calling birds, three French hens,
two turtle doves, and a partridge in a pear tree.

On the ninth day of Christmas my true love sent to me
Nine ladies dancing, eight maids a-milking, seven swans a-swimming,
six geese a-laying, five gold rings, four calling birds, three French hens,
two turtle doves, and a partridge in a pear tree.

On the tenth day of Christmas my true love sent to me
Ten lords a-leaping, nine ladies dancing, eight maids a-milking, seven
swans a-swimming, six geese a-laying, five gold rings, four calling birds,
three French hens, two turtle doves, and a partridge in a pear tree.

On the eleventh day of Christmas my true love sent to me
Eleven pipers piping, ten lords a-leaping, nine ladies dancing,
eight maids a-milking, seven swans a-swimming, six geese a-laying,
five gold rings, four calling birds, three French hens, two turtle doves,
and a partridge in a pear tree.

On the twelfth day of Christmas my true love sent to me
Twelve drummers drumming, eleven pipers piping, ten lords
a-leaping, nine ladies dancing, eight maids a-milking, seven swans
a-swimming, six geese a-laying, five gold rings, four calling birds,
three French hens, two turtle doves, and a partridge in a pear tree.

The Robin's Carol

On Christmas morning the snow was lying so thick that Mum said:

'David, go out and sweep the garden path, will you? Otherwise Grandma will never get to the door when she comes for Christmas lunch.'

David muttered and grumbled. He had just opened his presents and longed to play with his new computer game.

'Must I?' he said.

'Just think of poor Grandma struggling up the path in thick snow,' said Dad. 'She may fall down and hurt herself.'

David put on his old holey green sweater and his boots.

He got a long broom and began to sweep the path. It's not like Christmas at all, he thought. It could be any old day. People shouldn't have to *work* at Christmas.

Just then a little robin flew on to a twig nearby.

David looked at the robin sadly. 'How would *you* like it, Robin,' he said, 'if you were all warm and comfortable and ready for Christmas fun and you had to go out to sweep the path?'

Come to think of it, thought David, a robin is never warm and comfortable. He has to live outside all the time.

The little robin suddenly opened his beak and began to sing. And what a lovely song it was! A real Christmas carol! David cheered up immediately. If a little robin on a frozen twig could be cheerful, then so could he!

David set to work willingly. He swept a lovely clear path to the door, and then, tingling with the warmth that hard work brings, he went inside to enjoy the rest of Christmas.

Polly's Pets

Polly had two pet piglets. Father, who was a farmer, had wanted to send the two piglets to market, but Polly had pleaded and cried that she might be allowed to keep them for herself.

Father looked at her seriously. 'Pets are a responsibility,' he said. 'If you keep them you must look after them. You must prepare their food and clean out their sty and keep them clean.'

'Oh, *yes,*' said Polly eagerly. 'I will.'

It is very easy to make promises, but not so easy to keep them. While the late autumn days were still fine and warm it was no trouble for Polly to get up early, mix the piglets' food and take it out to the sty.

But just before Christmas it turned very very cold. Polly's hands were frozen blue when she scrubbed out the sty and washed the piglets.

'*Must* I?' she pleaded to her father.

'Who else do you suppose will do it?' replied Father. 'Of course I could send them to market...'

'Oh, *no,*' said Polly, and burst into tears. And off she went to feed her pets.

On Christmas morning when Polly woke up it was snowing. She shivered and looked longingly at her bulging stocking by the bed. But no, she had to go out to the piglets first.

Once she was back indoors again and as warm as toast Polly soon forgot her little pets in the sty. She had a wonderful Christmas Day with lots to eat and the sort of presents any child would wish for – a new dolls' pram, a toy fire-engine, a big fluffy dog you could cuddle and take to bed with you.

That evening Polly forgot about her piglets. She went to bed, tired, happy and very full of food.

Just as her eyes were closing Mother came into the room and asked:

'Have you seen to your piglets?'

Polly was beautifully snug and warm under her eiderdown. 'Mm,' she said sleepily, and Mother tiptoed away.

Next morning Polly woke early. Usually she slept while Father went out to milk the cows, but today something had woken her. It was a thin, squealing, unhappy sort of noise.

Then Polly remembered.

'My piglets!' she cried, and jumped out of bed. She was very worried.

Supposing one of the piglets had died in the night? Supposing Father was so angry that he would send both of them to market? They sounded very hungry and very miserable.

Polly ran downstairs, out of the back door and over to the pig-sty.

Two very indignant little piglets greeted her, shivering with cold. They weren't only hungry, they were thirsty too, because in the bitter cold their water bowl had frozen over. Polly broke the ice with a stone.

And do you know, those little piglets were so hungry that they followed Polly right to the kitchen door, squealing piteously as she prepared their mash.

Mother came into the kitchen and looked at the little shivering piglets. 'You didn't feed them last night, did you?' she said to Polly. '*You* had your lovely Christmas dinner, but what about these little mites?'

Mother went to the door and tenderly picked them up, one under each arm. 'I think they deserve a Christmas treat, don't you?' she said. 'How about letting them stay indoors by the kitchen stove? Just until the weather gets better?'

And Polly thought that this was a very, very good idea.

Christmas Decorations

'I love Christmas,' said Tim. 'All that holly and the Christmas tree.'

'It looks lovely,' agreed his father, admiring all the greenery around the room. 'But we aren't the only ones to produce Christmas decorations.'

'Of course not,' said Tim. 'There's Amanda – she has a wonderful tree – and Mark's got a real Nativity set, and –'

'That's not what I mean,' interrupted Father. 'I mean that Mother Nature has some Christmas surprises up her sleeve.'

Tim looked at his father in surprise. *'Really?'* he said.

Father was a schoolteacher. He liked telling Tim things. 'Come with me,' he said, taking Tim by the hand. They walked out into the frosty garden.

'Look over there,' said Father. 'Christmas roses. And that large bush with the sprays of yellow blossom is called mahonia.'

'And there are some holly berries,' added Tim. 'And winter jasmine.'

'Good,' said Father. 'Now you find me one more thing and I'll give you a present for the foot of your stocking.'

Tim walked all round the garden and suddenly gave a shout:

'Father! Look what I've found.'

There, in a corner of the garden gate, was an exquisite, lacy, frost-spangled cobweb.

'Clever spider,' said Tim.

When Tim opened his stocking on Christmas morning, there was a little square package in the toe. It was a small book called *Treasures of the Garden.*

A Present from Norway

At the bottom of a garden, on the edge of a forest in Norway, grew a fir-tree. Lars, Hilde, Nils and Solveig loved it very much, for they had watched it grow bigger and bigger each year. Long ago, it had been so small that their own father and his brother and sisters had decorated it like a real, indoor Christmas tree. Now it was too tall for that, though Nils would tie little silver ornaments on its bottom branches.

One day Lars was looking out of the window, and suddenly gave a cry of dismay:

'Oh, look!' he cried to his brother and sisters. 'They're cutting down our tree!'

Nils and Hilde ran downstairs. They pushed their feet into their boots and ran down the garden to the edge of the forest. Two men were standing by their tree, axes at the ready.

'You can't cut down our tree, you *can't,*' cried little Nils, tugging at one of the men's arms.

'Hold on, little one,' said the man, smiling. 'This tree is special, very special.'

The children stood quietly, listening to what the men had to say.

'This fir-tree is a present from the people of Norway to the people of Great Britain. It's to thank them for saving us during the last war.'

'When it's down,' went on the second man, 'it will be taken all the way to England. It will stand in Trafalgar Square, in the middle of London, and it will be decorated with hundreds of white lights. People from all over the world will sing carols under it. It will be famous!'

Their tree – famous! Lars, Hilde, Nils and Solveig felt very proud that their very own tree would go all those hundreds of miles to England.

'Tell you what,' said one of the men. 'My cousin lives in London. Shall I get him to take a photo of the tree to send back to you?'

The children nodded eagerly, though they felt a bit sad that they would never see their tree again except in a photograph. After that they hurried indoors so they wouldn't hear it being cut down.

'Did you see?' said Solveig. 'There's another little tree growing nearby. We'll be able to decorate it, just like Father did years ago.'

On New Year's Day a special letter fell on the mat, with English stamps on it.

'Our tree!' cried the children – and it was. A wonderful photograph of their tree, all shining with white lights and with a choir underneath singing carols.

King Wenceslaus

Long ago, in a country we now know as Czechoslovakia, there lived a good king called Wenceslaus. He was well loved by his subjects because of his kindness and his thought for the poor.

One winter's day on the Feast of St Stephen, which is what we now call Boxing Day, King Wenceslaus was looking out of his palace window. It was bitterly cold and the snow lay thick on the ground. Suddenly he called his page to him and pointed to a bent figure battling his way home through the snow.

'Who is that poor man?' he asked. 'He looks ill-clad for such freezing weather.'

'He is indeed poor, sire,' said the page. 'He lives in a shack near the Fountain of St Agnes. They say he is so poor that he cannot afford to buy the logs for his fire.'

The king ordered the page to the palace kitchens.

'Bring me some wine, bread and fruit,' he said, and a bundle of fire wood. We will go together to the Fountain of Saint Agnes to bring the poor man some Christmas cheer.'

It was terribly cold as the king and his page set forth. They had not got far from the palace when the young page began to falter.

'I cannot go on, sire,' he whimpered. 'My feet are so cold that I can no longer feel them, and my hands too.'

'You *must* go on,' ordered the king severely. 'Think of that poor man who has no food or heat. Follow behind me in my footsteps and you'll find your feet feel warmer.'

It was as the king said. As soon as the page put his small feet into the king's big footprints he felt them tingling and coming to life again. Very soon he was as warm as toast.

As for the poor man the king and his page visited, why he never forgot that Christmas and the kindness of King Wenceslaus in his hour of need.

Silent Night

Silent night, holy night,
All is calm, all is bright;
Round yon virgin, Mother and Child,
Holy Infant, so tender and mild,
Sleep in heavenly peace,
Sleep in heavenly peace.

Silent night, holy night,
Shepherds quake at the sight;
Glories stream from Heaven afar,
Heavenly hosts sing Alleluia;
Christ the Saviour is born!
Christ the Saviour is born!

Silent night, holy night,
Son of God, love's pure light,
Radiant beams from Thy holy face,
With the dawn of redeeming grace,
Jesus, Lord, at Thy birth,
Jesus, Lord, at Thy birth.

Tree in the Moonlight

Charlotte woke first. 'Psst,' she said to Emma and Jack. 'I can hear Mama and Papa preparing the Christmas tree.'

It was Christmas Eve. In those days most families waited until the night before Christmas before dressing the tree.

Jack jumped out of bed and listened at the door. He could hear the rustle of the tissue paper as their parents took the precious glass ornaments out of the box. He could almost hear the tinkle of the little silver bells.

'I know,' said Emma suddenly. 'Let's go down to look at the tree after Mama and Papa have gone to bed.'

'We could open our presents, too,' said Jack excitedly. Charlotte shook him hard.

'No, you can't! Whatever would our parents say tomorrow morning!'

But the temptation of slipping down the stairs at midnight to look at the big tree standing in the hall all covered with glass balls, bells and tinsel was too good to be missed.

'We must go quietly, mind,' said Charlotte, who was the oldest and the most sensible. They waited until they heard Mama and Papa climb the stairs to bed, and then they dressed hurriedly - it was far too cold to go down in their night clothes.

They stole quietly down the twisty stairs which led to the big square hall.

'I'm *scared*,' said little Jack, holding Charlotte tightly by the hand. As they turned the corner of the staircase and came into the hall, they gasped with delight.

The moon was very bright. It shone on the silver bells and the golden birds, on the threads of tinsel on the branches, and on the angel at the very topmost tip of the tree. Below, in the shadows, the children could see large lumpy parcels.

Jack longed to rush over to open them, but Charlotte held him firmly.

'Oh, I'm *glad* we came,' breathed Emma. 'It's different in the moonlight. The angel looks as if she's got a halo.'

The three of them stood there for ages, quietly holding hands. The tree seemed magical on this most holy of nights, all silvery and mysterious.

Then Charlotte gave the two young ones a little push, and they started back to bed again. When they reached the staircase Jack just sat down

on the bottom step and refused to move.

'I don't want to go to bed,' he complained. 'Can't I just open one tiny weeny little parcel?'

'No you can't,' snapped Charlotte. 'It would be quite wrong, like stealing from church.'

It had been rather like church standing in the big hall in front of the magical tree, just as they would often stand by the crib beside the altar. It would have been quite, quite wrong to touch the presents.

'Come *on*, Jack,' she said. 'It's after one o'clock.' She dragged Jack upstairs to the bedroom.

Jack soon forgot his disappointment over not being allowed to open a present. All that remained was a wonderful vision of the tree, with the bright angel on top and the rustly, silvery branches. He went to sleep with a big smile on his face. The presents were still there, to look forward to in the morning.

The Christmas Crib

When the children walked into the church with their mother they went straight up the aisle to the Christmas crib which stood underneath the tall Christmas tree at the side of the altar. It was beautiful. There were Mary and Joseph and the angels, the wise men and the shepherds, with a shiny star hanging above them.

'Does every church have a crib?' asked James.

'Most do,' said Mother. 'It's to remind us of that first Christmas. Would you like me to tell you about the very first Christmas crib?'

The children nodded eagerly, and Mother began:

'Long ago there lived a man called St Francis. We know of him because of the love he had for all animals, but he was also said to have given the people of the village of Greccio in Italy a very special gift.

One Christmas Eve the people of the little village came out of their houses to celebrate mass as usual, and there they found that St Francis had presented them with a real manger with sheep and cattle standing round it. St Francis stood in front of the manger, reading the Christmas story. A woman, who was carrying her baby in her arms, laid him gently in the manger, and as the stars shone down on the little scene the people of Greccio could see how it had been

in Bethlehem all those hundreds of years ago.

Since that time most churches have a Christmas crib. A miniature manger, a tiny child, Mary, Joseph, and all the shepherds, gather round so that people today can remember and celebrate the birth of Christ.'

St Nicholas

Did you know that Santa Claus was a real person who lived many hundreds of years ago in place called Myra, which is now in Turkey. He was a bishop, and his real name was St Nicholas. He was known for the quiet and generous ways in which he helped people, slipping away quickly before anyone realised who he was.

At that time in Myra there lived three unmarried sisters. They were unmarried because they could not afford the dowries that girls needed to give to their future husbands. A dowry was a large sum of money. Now these three sisters had not a penny to rub between them, and so they saw little chance of ever getting married. Indeed the eldest sister did have a sweetheart, but she could never see the day when he would become her husband.

One evening the eldest sister suddenly heard a small sound outside the door. She hurried to open it, and there, on the porch, was a bag of money. Whoever had left it, though, had hurried away, leaving no note or letter to give away his or her identity. Of course the girl was now able to marry her young man, but this was not the end of the story. Before long both her sisters had also been left handsome dowries, yet were unable to find out who their kind friend was, though the youngest girl had caught a glimpse of a red cloak and a tall hat slipping away into the trees. We, of course, know that the stranger was St Nicholas.

Throughout the ages St Nicholas has changed a bit. His red bishop's cloak has become a red coat, trimmed with white fur, and his tall mitre a red hood. 'Santa Claus' is an abbreviation of St Nicholas. Dutch children first called him Sante Klaas when they used to put out their clogs to receive his gifts each Christmas.

But whether we know him as St Nicholas or Santa Claus he represents for all children everywhere the true loving and giving spirit of Christmas.

The Mistletoe Kiss

Meg, Peter and little Henry were collecting greenery for the Christmas decorations. Their father had already dug up a splendid tree, and the children had helped him carry it home. Now they were out looking for holly. *Crunch, crunch, crunch* went their feet through the snow and into the silent woods. The holly was not hard to find, though prickly to pick. Soon they had a big bunch of it. They were just starting back home again when Meg suddenly stopped.

'We've forgotten the mistletoe,' she cried. All three children knew that the mistletoe was important. Their big brother Oliver was bringing his sweetheart home for Christmas, and everyone wanted to see him give Elizabeth a kiss under the mistletoe.

Mistletoe is a funny plant. It doesn't grow into bushes and trees like holly. You find it growing on the bough of another tree, where a bird has planted its seed. Meg, Peter and Henry looked and looked for ages, and it was just beginning to get dark when Peter spotted it, high on the branch of an apple tree.

'It's too high for me to reach it,' cried Meg, who was the eldest and tallest.

'But Henry can if you lift him,' said Peter.

And Henry could just touch the nearest leaf. He pulled at it so that the spray of mistletoe was low enough for Meg to pick. It was now nearly completely dark.

'Wherever have you been?' cried Mother, as the children came home.

'Finding a kiss for Oliver,' laughed Peter. 'A mistletoe kiss!'

I Saw Three Ships

I saw three ships come sailing in,
On Christmas Day, on Christmas Day,
I saw three ships come sailing in,
On Christmas Day in the morning.

And what was in those ships all three?
On Christmas Day, on Christmas Day,
And what was in those ships all three?
On Christmas Day in the morning.

Our Saviour Christ and his lady,
On Christmas Day, on Christmas Day
Our Saviour Christ and his lady,
On Christmas Day in the morning.

Pray whither sailed those ships all three?
On Christmas Day, on Christmas Day,
Pray whither sailed those ships all three?
On Christmas Day in the morning.

O they sailed into Bethlehem,
On Christmas Day, on Christmas Day,
O they sailed into Bethlehem,
On Christmas Day in the morning.

And all the bells on earth shall ring,
On Christmas Day, on Christmas Day,
And all the bells on earth shall ring,
On Christmas Day in the morning.

And all the angels in Heaven shall sing,
On Christmas Day, on Christmas Day,
And all the angels in Heaven shall sing,
On Christmas Day in the morning.

And all the souls on earth shall sing,
On Christmas Day, on Christmas Day,
And all the souls on earth shall sing,
On Christmas Day in the morning.

Then let us all rejoice amain!
On Christmas Day, on Christmas Day,
Then let us all rejoice amain!
On Christmas Day in the morning.

37

The Christmas Surprise

'I'm afraid there won't be any Christmas cheer this year,' said Mother. The six children stared at her in dismay.

'No Christmas! No presents or turkey or Christmas Tree!'

Mother looked at their disappointed faces and sighed.

'I'm sorry,' she said. 'But with Papa so ill in hospital and not much money, I don't think it would be right. Perhaps when Papa's better we'll have a *late* Christmas.'

Little Susie pouted and began to cry. 'It's not the *same*. It's not right not having Christmas on 25th December.'

But Mother wasn't listening. She began to put some fresh fruit into a basket to take to the hospital for their father.

All six children wandered out into the street. Everything looked gloomy. There was a little house on the corner where their old friend, Mrs Lacey used to live. But now she had gone to live with her daughter, because she was very old and frail. The little house stood empty and dark. It expressed exactly what the children were feeling.

'Poor Papa,' said James. 'We mustn't forget how awful it is for him, stuck in hospital at Christmas.'

Just as the children reached the corner a funny thing thing happened. A light came on in the little house. The door opened. On the step stood Mrs Lacey's daughter. She smiled at them all.

'Dear me, you look gloomy,' she said.

Susie burst into tears. 'We're not having Christmas this year,' she wailed.

'We can't have that,' said Mrs Lacey's daughter. 'Do you know why we've come back?'

The children shook their heads.

'Mother was homesick for Christmas in her own little house. So we've come back to warm it up and spend one last Christmas here before we sell. It's not really Christmas though without children, so how would you like to come along here on Christmas evening?'

'Oh *yes*,' they chorused.

On Christmas afternoon Mother set off for the hospital to visit Papa, and the children ran down the street to the little house on the corner.

What a lovely surprise! In the lighted window stood a little Christmas tree, its lights ablaze. The children gasped in wonder at the welcoming sight.

'Come on in, my dears,' said Mrs Lacey's daughter, and old Mrs Lacey was sitting in a chair, smiling a welcome. There was a regular Christmas feast, and a present for each of them, too.

But the best present of all was when Mother returned to say Papa was coming home the very next week!

Away in a Manger

Away in a manger, no crib for a bed,
The little Lord Jesus laid down His sweet head;
The stars in the bright sky looked down where He lay,
The little Lord Jesus asleep on the hay.

The cattle are lowing, the baby awakes;
But little Lord Jesus, no crying He makes;
I love thee, Lord Jesus! Look down from the sky,
And stay by my bedside till morning is nigh.

Be near me, Lord Jesus; I ask Thee to stay
Close by me for ever, and love me, I pray:
Bless all the dear children in Thy tender care,
And fit us for Heaven to live with Thee there.

Lucy's Mistake

Every year Lucy's mother and father would buy a splendid Christmas tree and every year Lucy would be allowed to decorate it with all the coloured glass ornaments Mother kept in a big cardboard box.

One year something terrible happened. Mother was just taking the box of decorations from the top shelf of the cupboard where it was stored when it slipped from her hand. There was an awful smashing and tinkling sound, and when Lucy opened the box all the precious ornaments were broken to smithereens.

'Oh, oh,' cried Lucy and burst into tears.

Mother always liked looking on the bright side of things. 'Never mind,' she said. 'Though it's too late and too expensive to replace the ornaments, I have a very good idea. How about collecting some fir-cones and painting them silver? You could find some holly berries, too, and thread them on strings.'

Lucy remembered that she sometimes helped Mother make biscuits with a star-shaped pastry cutter. 'We could make some star biscuits with silver balls on,' she said.

Very soon the tragedy of the glass ornaments was forgotten. After all, it was far more exciting to make your own Christmas decorations.

While Lucy's biscuits were baking away in the oven she went out into the garden to look for fir-cones and holly berries. Suddenly her eyes caught sight of something else sparkling in the trees.

'They're pretty!' she exclaimed, and reached up to pick them. They were very cold to the touch. I could tie them with thread and hang them from the branches, thought Lucy.

Later Mother came into the room to admire the tree. Lucy came in after her, with a tray of perfectly-shaped little star biscuits decorated with silver balls.

'Oh, where are my lovely ornaments?' wailed Lucy, looking at the tree.

'And where's all this water come from?' asked Mother.

Poor Lucy! She had picked some icicles, not thinking that they would melt in the heat of the house. 'How silly of me,' she said, blushing red.

Mother smiled brightly, as she always did. 'Never mind, Lucy,' she said. 'I've found something nearly as good at the back of the cupboard.'

And she brought out some long silvery strands of tinsel to adorn the tree.

The Christmas Parcel Disaster

Charles and Paula's cousins lived right at the other end of the village. Every Christmas Eve Mama would wrap up all their presents, ready for the children to take over to them. Mother was especially good at wrapping parcels. They always looked neat and pretty.

'Why do *my* parcels always look all battered and untidy,' complained Paula, as she watched her mother tie a beautiful bow of blue ribbon.

'It's because you are so impatient,' laughed Mama. 'You have to do things slowly and with care.'

At last the parcels were all ready. Charles and Paula held out their arms, while Mama piled the presents into them.

'Are you sure you can manage?' she asked anxiously.

'Of *course* we can,' said Charles. 'They are quite small and not very heavy.'

'May we take Fifi?' asked Paula. Fifi was their little dog.

'If you keep her under control,' said Mama. 'I don't want you tripping up over her.'

Mama watched as the two children set off down the village street. 'Keep to the road,' she called after them, but they pretended not to hear.

'I say,' said Paula, as they reached the village pond. 'Let's take a short cut over the ice. It's completely frozen over and it will save us having to walk round the edge.'

'It looks horribly slippery,' remarked Charles, nervously putting a toe on the ice.

'Oh, come *on,*' said Paula impatiently, 'or we'll never get there!'

Both children set off across the pond, Fifi skidding and sliding along beside them.

'Don't go so quickly,' cried Charles. 'You're pushing me!'

Too late! Paula slipped, and clutched at Charles's arm to save herself. Fifi somehow got mixed up under their feet, and all the presents flew into the air.

All three of them landed in a heap in the middle of the pond. Luckily for them the ice was thick and did not crack.

'Was there anything breakable in the parcels?' asked Paula in a small voice. She knew it had all been her fault. She had been too impatient to walk round the pond in the proper way.

Charles carefully retrieved all the parcels and shook them. 'Nothing sounds broken,' he said. 'But they look awfully messy.'

Paula's eyes filled with tears. All Mama's hard work was for nothing. The cousins would never see her beautiful bows and the pretty patterns on the paper. Every parcel was covered with dirt and water.

'I'll never ever try to rush things again,' vowed Paula, and the little trio continued on their Christmas trip to the cousins' house.

Martin Luther and the Candles

Martin Luther was a great religious leader who lived in Germany several hundred years ago.

One bright frosty December night Luther was travelling home through the forest. The stars shone through the blackness of the trees, touching their branches with silver.

'Like heaven shining through the blackness,' he thought.

When he arrived home he dug up a little fir tree and covered its boughs with candles. He lit each candle and his children gasped with delight at the sight of the shining tree.

'That is what I wanted to share with you,' said Martin Luther. 'That is how it appeared to me as I walked through the forest under a starry sky – the night when the brightness of Heaven visited Earth.'

Once in Royal David's City

Once in royal David's city
Stood a lowly cattle shed,
Where a mother laid her baby
In a manger for his bed;
Mary was that mother mild,
Jesus Christ her little child.

He came down to earth from Heaven
Who is God and Lord of all,
And His shelter was a stable,
And His cradle was a stall;
With the poor, and mean, and lowly,
Lived on earth our Saviour holy.

And, through all His wondrous
   childhood,
He would honour and obey,
Love, and watch the lowly maiden,
In whose gentle arms he lay;
Christian children all must be
Mild, obedient, good as He.

For He is our childhood's pattern,
Day by day like us He grew,
He was little, weak and helpless,
Tears and smiles like us He knew;
And He feeleth for our sadness.
And He shareth in our gladness.

And our eyes at last shall see Him,
Through His own redeeming love,
For that Child so dear and gentle,
Is our Lord in Heav'n above;
And He leads his children on
To the place where He is gone.

Not in that poor lowly stable,
With the oxen standing by,
We shall see Him; but in Heaven,
Set at God's right hand on high;
When like stars His children crown'd
All in white shall wait around.

The Birds' Christmas

It was Sparrow who noticed it first – a long, straight pole sticking out of the middle of the lawn.

'What can it be?' wondered the birds.

'Well, it isn't a tree for a fact,' said Blackbird. 'It hasn't any branches.'

'And it isn't a telegraph pole,' said Starling. 'For there are no wires on top.'

'Perhaps it's a Christmas present for Woodpecker,' said Robin. 'So that he can bore holes in it.'

The birds didn't think much of this idea. Why should Woodpecker get a Christmas present and not the rest of them? After all, they had all sung their songs and pleased the humans during the year. Why did the humans give each other presents but only thought of giving one to Woodpecker and not the rest of the birds?

They were all gathered, pecking up crumbs from the edge of the lawn. It was quite dangerous, because Cat was often prowling nearby in the bushes.

'Scatter!' yelled Starling in her harsh voice, as Cat suddenly emerged from the hydrangea bush, claws and eyes flashing.

'It's no fun eating in this garden,' complained Chaffinch. 'And what will happen in the spring when the babies arrive I dread to think. *They* can't fly away quickly.'

The next morning was Christmas Day. It was freezing cold. Blackbird perched in a tree in the garden and suddenly exclaimed, 'Look at the pole!'

All the birds gathered on the bough to see what had happened.

The pole had a square platform on top, and a little roof. The birds could see several things dangling from the platform.

Robin flew to investigate. 'Come down, all of you,' he called to the other birds. 'You should see all the *food.*'

There on the bird-table (for that, of course, was what it was) lay a regular feast. There were bacon rinds and nuts and pieces of bread. There was a bowl of sunflower seeds. And from the table dangled more goodies – a half-coconut and two string bags of peanuts.

'Our Christmas present,' chirruped Sparrow.

'We can eat safe from Cat,' said Chaffinch in relief.

Then Robin sang a little carol outside the windows of the house to say, 'Thank you, Merry Christmas!'

God Rest You Merry, Gentlemen

God rest you merry, gentlemen,
Let nothing you dismay,
Remember Christ our Saviour
Was born on Christmas Day,
To save us all from Satan's power
When we were gone astray:

O tidings of comfort and joy,
*   comfort and joy,*
O tidings of comfort and joy.

In Bethlehem, in Jewry,
This blessed Babe was born,
And laid within a manger,
Upon this blessed morn;
To which His Mother Mary
Did nothing take in scorn:

From God our Heavenly Father
A blessed angel came;
And unto certain shepherds
Brought tidings of the same;
How that in Bethlehem was born
The Son of God by name:

Fear not, then said the angel,
Let nothing you affright,
This day is born a Saviour
Of a pure Virgin bright,
So frequently to vanquish all
The fiends of Satan quite:

The shepherds at those tidings
Rejoicèd much in mind,
And left their flocks a-feeding,
In tempest, storm and wind;
And went to Bethlehem
straightway,
This blessed Babe to find:

And when they came to Bethlehem
Where our dear Saviour lay,
They found Him in a manger,
Where oxen feed on hay;
His Mother Mary kneeling down,
Unto the Lord did pray:

Now to the Lord sing praises,
All you within this place,
And with true love and brotherhood
Each other now embrace;
The holy tide of Christmas
All other doth deface:

The Magic Toyshop

It was a wonderful toyshop. It had an old-fashioned bow-fronted window and the owner, Mr Jolly, was as cheerful as his name.

No child in the town would pass the shop without looking in the window, because Mr Jolly changed the display every week. One week the theme might be teddy-bears, another spaceships. One time Mr Jolly had a wooden ark in the window, and Mr Noah had over fifty different animals to go in it.

The best treat came at Christmas. Then Mr Jolly would create something every bit as good as the grand displays in the big shops. One year it had been Fairyland, and last year there had been a train set, complete with snowy landscape and little warmly wrapped figures standing at chilly stations. There were even some miniature snowmen.

This particular Christmas six children stopped by the window to see what surprise Mr Jolly had prepared for them.

'Oh, look!' said David. 'It's a dolls' Christmas party!'

And so it was. Every kind of toy was there – teddy-bears, clowns, Sindy dolls, Action Man, toy rabbits, cats, lions and dogs. There was a little Christmas tree, whose branches were covered with the kind of tiny toys and trinkets you would find in your Christmas stockings. There was a table of toy food – plaster cakes and little china cups and saucers. The children looked and looked, each moment discovering something else.

Then something dreadful happened. The little Christmas tree caught fire. One of the tiny light bulbs must have exploded.

'What shall we do?' wailed Samantha. The shop was shut and by the time the children had run for Mr Jolly, the whole window display would be ablaze.

'Look,' cried Jane, clutching at her brother John's arm. To the children's amazement a whole toy fire-brigade rushed into the window from the back of the shop, brandishing toy hoses. They turned on the hoses, and real water gushed out. Within seconds the fire was out. Everything was exactly as it had been before, except that the little tree's lights had gone out.

'There's no such thing as magic,' scoffed Gemma. 'We must have imagined it happened.'

'Did we?' asked David. The children looked carefully at the display. Where the fire had first started, halfway up the tree, was a bare space with blackened twigs. And some of the toys who had been standing looking at the table laden with food were now facing the tree.

'Enjoy your party,' said the children, waving to all the toys.

And the toys waved back!

Here We Come A-Wassailing

Here we come a-wassailing
Among the leaves so green,
Here we come a-wandering,
So fair to be seen:

Love and joy come to you
And to you your wassail too,
And God bless you and send you
A happy New Year,
And God send you a happy New Year.

Our wassail cup is made,
Of the rosemary tree,
And so is your beer
Of the best barley:

We are not daily beggars
That beg from door to door,
But we are neighbours' children
Whom you have seen before:

Call up the butler of this house,
Put on his golden ring;
Let him bring us up a glass of beer,
And better shall we sing:

We have got a little purse
Of ratching leather skin;
We want a little of your money
To line it well within:

Bring us out a table,
And spread it with a cloth;
Bring us out a mouldy cheese,
And some of your Christmas loaf:

God bless the master of this house,
Likewise the mistress too;
And all the little children
That round the table go:

Jack Frost

Of all the Elements in the House of Weather Jack Frost was the most unhappy.

'Nobody loves me,' he complained. 'I shrivel up the flowers and people shiver when I'm around and say, "Brrh, how I *hate* the cold!"

'People hate me sometimes,' said Rain.

'But the farmers like you – and the ducks. People like Snow, too, they can build snowmen. And children love Wind – they can fly their kites. But *nobody* likes me,' said Jack Frost.

That Christmas Eve, Jack Frost crept out of the House of Weather and touched the ground with his sparkly feet. He reached up and stroked the tree boughs, and he looked into warm and friendly homes with holly and garlands and Christmas trees.

'As it's Christmas I'll do something special,' said Jack Frost. 'The windows of the house could be decorated too. Then perhaps people will love me.'

Jack Frost worked all night, tracing delicate patterns with his icy fingers. And because it was still very cold on Christmas morning Jack Frost stayed near the houses to hear what people said.

Little Rachel was ill in bed. She cried herself to sleep at the thought of missing all the Christmas goodies. When she woke and looked out of the window she gasped with delight.

'Patterns!' she cried. 'Flowers and silver leaves. How beautiful.' And immediately she felt better.

It was the same everywhere. Jack Frost went from house to house hearing people praising his frosty decorations. He felt very good indeed. It was a wonderful feeling to be loved at last – especially at Christmas.

The Young King's Gift

There was once a young king who felt himself to be unworthy of his position. He had lands and riches, he had armies and weapons, but he often wished that he could lead a simpler, more peaceful life. He didn't like fighting, or wars, and he felt guilty at owning so much when many people lived in dire poverty.

One day the young king heard a strange rumour. A new star had appeared in the east and it was said that this star was special, that it heralded the birth of a great king.

The young king went outside his palace and looked up into the sky. Sure enough, a new star shone more brightly than any other in the starry firmament.

There was another rumour. The new king had been born in a manger, the son of a poor village girl.

The young king looked round his palace and opened his store of treasure.

'A new and important king, yet he is so poor and I am so rich. He must be someone very special if he has a star to herald his birth.'

That night the young king set forth. He travelled alone, save for his faithful wolfhounds, and he wore a circlet of gold which was his crown.

He travelled for many hundreds of miles until he came to Bethlehem in Judea. Everything was exactly as had been rumoured. There was the simple manger and there the young girl with her husband keeping watch over the baby.

The young king approached the manger and went down on bended knee. 'Great king,' he said. 'I give you my riches and my power, for neither is of use to me. You can become a great king, and I will give up my kingdom to you.'

So saying he held out his sword and his golden crown, and offered them to the new king.

The baby was tiny, yet the young king heard His voice speaking to him. 'My kingdom is not of this earth. You have strength yet you prefer peace. You have riches yet you would live simply. Now go out into the world as I will do shortly, and give all you have to the poor. For of such people is the kingdom of Heaven made.'

In the Bleak Midwinter

In the bleak midwinter Frosty wind
made moan,
Earth stood hard as iron, Water like a stone;
Snow had fallen, snow on snow,
Snow on snow,
In the bleak midwinter, Long ago.

Our God, heav'n cannot hold him
Nor earth sustain;
Heav'n and earth shall flee away
When he comes to reign;
In the bleak midwinter
A Stable place sufficed
The Lord God Almighty
Jesus Christ.

Acknowledgements

The illustrations on pages 1, 3, 7, 11, 13,
17, 18, 22, 24, 25, 26, 28, 31, 33, 34, 36, 39, 41,
43, 49, 50, 52, 53 & 55 are reproduced by kind
permission of Royle Publications Limited, London.